An Illustrated Guide to

Mythical Creatures

A wondrous introduction to the varied life-forms of hearsay found in the myths, legends, and folklore of cultures around the world.

Illustrations by David West   Text by Anita Ganeri

Published in 2009 by

David West ⚇ Children's Books
7 Princeton Court
55 Felsham Road
London SW15 1AZ

First edition 2009

11 10 09
10 9 8 7 6 5 4 3 2 1

ISBN-13: 978-0-9553477-3-3

Designed and illustrated by David West
Written by Anita Ganeri and David West

Photo Credits:
12tr, Hector Joseph Lumang; 12bl, Lynn Watson; 43ml, Sander Kamp; 43br, David Evans

Printed and bound in China.

Contents

Introduction

Herein lies a magical world of strange creatures and fabulous beasts, where the Cockatrice's glance can turn a person to stone and the trumpet of the Manticore lures unsuspecting travelers to their doom. Here are knights riding Hippogriffs, heroes battling fire-breathing dragons, Scorpion men guarding the tombs of the dead, and giants fighting gods.

Dare to turn the pages of this book to discover a world of myth and legend beyond your most fanciful dreams!

A knight battles a dragon to rescue a maiden.

Dragons, Serpents, & Worms

Here be dragons... Dragons appear in almost every mythology around the world, as immense, lizard-like beasts covered in scales. They hatch from eggs after thousands of years, and are sometimes said to spit poison or breathe fire.

Y Ddraig Gosh, the Welsh red dragon

Dragons East and West

As with most creatures of myth, dragons are understood and depicted in different ways by different cultures. Eastern dragons—most notably from China and Japan—are very powerful but usually benevolent. They are revered for their great wisdom and are often worshipped as mythical rulers of nature and the weather, particularly of water and rain. Unlike Western dragons, these dragons do not have wings because it is believed that they fly by magic.

In the mythologies of the West, most dragons are dangerous. Some live in caves where they fiercely guard hoards of gold and treasure. Others terrorize towns and villages, demanding human sacrifices to eat. Unlike Eastern dragons, there are numerous legends of these terrible beasts being hunted down and killed.

In Eastern mythology, the Azure Dragon is one of the four symbols of the constellation. It represents the East, spring, and the element of wood.

One of the most famous dragon slayers of Christian folklore is St. George, shown in the 15th-century Russian icon above. Legend says that he killed a dragon that was about to devour the king's daughter.

Eastern dragons, like the one in this Japanese dragon shrine, are often shown with a large pearl in their grasp, though some say that it is really the dragon's egg.

Dragon slayers are famous and heroic characters in Western folklore. In Greek mythology, Prince Cadmus is sent in search of his missing sister, Europa. He fails to find her but decides to found a city on a spot guarded by a serpentlike dragon, which he kills. In medieval times, there were many famous dragon slayers like Siegfried, hero of the German epoch poem Niebelungenlied. He kills the dragon, Fafnir, and drinks its blood. This makes him invulnerable, apart from one small spot on his shoulder.

Wyverns are said to be more aggressive
than dragons and to prey on humans and livestock.

Wyverns and Lindworms

Although it has similarities to a
European dragon, the legendary
Wyvern differs in having only two
legs, with large wings instead of
front limbs, and sometimes with
eagle's claws on the tips. It is unsure
whether Wyverns breathe fire, like
dragons, but they have deadly arrow-
shaped barbs at the ends of their tails
for killing their prey. In medieval
Europe, Wyverns were associated with
war, pestilence, and plague. Today,
images of them can be seen as heraldic emblems
on arms, crests, and flags—usually as a symbol
of strength and endurance. Wyverns are closely
related to Lindworms, which appear in Scandinavian
and German mythology. Lindworms are often
described as having the body of a serpent and a
poisonous bite. These enormous and terrifying
beasts eat cattle and are believed to raid
churchyards to devour the dead.

*The Zilant, a
Wyvern, is the
official emblem
of Kazan,
Russia.*

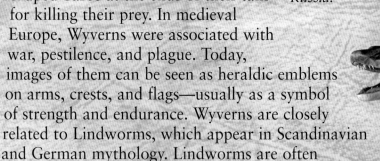

Worms

In northern European mythology, the word for dragon
is *worm*, which means "snake or serpent." In old
English, it is "wyrm." Legends from the Middle Ages
describe Worms as serpents with no wings or legs but with
dragons' heads. One of the best-known tales of this creature
is of the Lambton Worm. It tells how young John Lambton
catches a Worm while fishing in the local river, and then
throws it down a nearby well. Over the years, the beast grows
to a huge size and attacks the local livestock
and villagers. John Lambton strikes a bargain with a witch, who
gives him the power to slay the beast. However, when he
is unable to fulfill his end of the deal, she
puts a curse on his family.

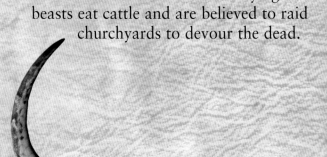

*John Lambton
fought the Worm
by a river. The
water carried
away the pieces
of the beast
before they
could join up
to re-form its
body.*

Feathered Serpent

For thousands of years, Quetzalcoatl,
the feathered serpent, was one of
the most important characters in
Aztec
mythology,
religion, and art.
Often depicted as a snake with a
headdress made from quetzal
bird feathers, Quetzalcoatl was
also the wind god, the patron god of priests, and
believed to be responsible for the creation of the world.

*Quetzalcoatl
devouring a man,
from an ancient
manuscript*

8

Many-headed Serpents

In Ancient Greek legend, the hero Heracles (Hercules) is given the task of killing the Hydra, a huge snake with numerous heads, and breath so poisonous it can kill human beings. On reaching Lake Lerna, the home of the beast, Heracles faces off with the Hydra and attempts to strike it down. But each time Heracles cuts off one of its heads, two more heads grow in its place. Heracles calls on his nephew Ioalus for help. After each head is cut off, Ioalus seals the stump with a burning branch until, at last, the Hydra is dead. In a later task, Heracles also kills the hundred-headed serpent, Ladon, which guards the Garden of Hesperides, in order to steal the apples of immortality.

The Garden of Hesperides, painted by Frederic Leighton

Heracles battles Hydra, the many-headed serpent

Giant Serpents

Many cultures have myths describing giant serpents that do battle with the gods. These conflicts often represent the struggle of good versus evil, as in the Ancient Egyptian myth of Apep. Apep is a giant serpent that represents darkness and chaos and is therefore the archenemy of order and light. Every night, as the sun god, Ra, sinks below the horizon, he does battle with Apep in the underworld but always returns victorious in the morning to the sky.

In Norse mythology, Jormungandr is so enormous that he encircles Midgard (the world of humans) under the ocean and holds his own tail in his mouth. He is greatly feared by sailors who venture into the deep waters where he lives. Jormungandr's archenemy is Thor, the god of thunder. One story tells how Thor goes fishing with a giant called Hymir. As Thor rows further out to sea, Hymir warns him that they are in danger. Thor ignores the giant's warning and casts his line, baited with an ox's head, which Jormungandr snatches. After a great struggle, Thor pulls the serpent from the water and is about to kill him when Hymir cuts the line and it escapes. Thor and Jormundgandr are destined to meet again at Ragnarok (the battle that destroys the world), when Thor will kill the serpent only to fall dead from Jormungandr's poison.

A painting of Thor fighting the Midgard serpent, by Henry Fuseli

An Ancient Egyptian painting showing a god warding off the serpent Apep

Roger rides a Hippogriff to rescue Angelique.

Flying Creatures

Folk tales, myths, legends, and heraldry are filled with examples of fantastical flying creatures and winged beasts. None is more majestic than the fabulous Griffin, with the body of a lion and the head and wings of an eagle.

An illustration of a Griffin by Sir John Tenniel for Lewis Carroll's *Alice in Wonderland*

A Peryton

The Simurgh

Part Bird...

Tales of Griffins reached Europe from ancient Scythia where these legendary beasts were said to line their nests with gold, killing anyone who dared steal it from them. In medieval times, it was believed that a Griffin's feathers and claws had magical powers. The feathers were thought to cure blindness. A cup made from a Griffin claw could warn of the presence of poison by changing color. Even rarer than the Griffin was the Hippogriff, the offspring of a Griffin and a horse. Hippogriffs were extremely rare because Griffins and horses were archenemies.

Another mythical birdlike beast was the Peryton, which has the forelegs, head, and antlers of a stag, and the wings, feathers, and back legs of a bird. Said to come from the legendary land of Atlantis, the Peryton casts the shadow of a man.

In Persian mythology, the Simurgh is a bird with a dog's head and a lion's claws. Its wings are so huge that they could block out the sun. It is said to have lived for so long that it is the keeper of all knowledge.

One of the most famous flying creatures of all is Pegasus, the winged horse of ancient Greek mythology who carries the hero, Bellerophon, to kill the Chimera (see page 17). A similar winged horse, known as Buraq, appears in Islamic literature and art.

Buraq, from a 17th-century Mughal drawing

Pegasus and Bellerophon

Other Winged Creatures

The Hsigo, or Hsaio, is a monkey with wings that appears in Chinese folklore. Its presence is believed to warn of serious drought. The legend of the Hsigo may have inspired the flying monkeys in the book *The Wonderful Wizard of Oz*. Human-headed lions and bulls, called Shedu or Lamassu, come from Ancient Assyria. Sculptures of these creatures were placed as guardians at the entrances of cities and palaces.

Hsigos in flight

Harpies and Sirens

Birdlike creatures with human heads appear in mythology throughout the world. Among the most terrible are the Harpies of Ancient Greece. They torment humans by stealing their food and screeching so that their victims cannot eat or rest. It was said that the only thing they were frightened of was the sound made by a brass instrument.

Sirens look similar to Harpies, but Greek stories tell how they used their beautiful singing voices to lure sailors to their deaths on the rocks. In Russian mythology, they were known as Sirins, and were equally dangerous. Humans who heard their song left everything behind to follow them, ultimately to their death.

Sirin (left) and Alkonost, birds of joy and sorrow, by Vicktor Vasnetsov (1896)

A sculpture of a Lamassu from Ancient Assyria

In this 1891 painting by John William Waterhouse, the Greek hero Odysseus, tied to the mast, survives the Sirens' song. On the advice of an enchantress, he blocks his men's ears with beeswax so that they cannot hear their fateful singing.

Giant Birds

The Roc was an enormous mythical bird so strong that it was believed to be able to carry off elephants and eat them. From the Middle East, the legend of the Roc reached the West through Marco Polo's account of his travels and in the book *The 1001 Nights*, which included the story of Sinbad the Sailor. The Roc may have been inspired by the elephant bird of Madagascar, which became extinct in the 16th century.

Other legends include Vucub-Cacquix ("Seven Macaw"), the giant Mayan bird-demon that claimed to be the sun and the moon; the Chinese Peng that could fly for six months without resting; and the Ziz from Hebrew mythology, which had wings that could block out the sun.

In The 1001 Nights, *Sinbad the Sailor's ship is destroyed by a Roc.*

A Phoenix painted on the walls of a tower in Tian Hou Temple, Shenzhen, Guangdon, China

Fire and Thunder Birds

In Native North American legend, the Thunderbird is a mythical bird of immense power and strength. It is believed that lightning flashes from its eyes and that the beating of its huge wings causes the sound of thunder. Similarly, the South African Impundulu, or "lightning bird," is a black and white bird, the size of a human, which summons thunder and lightning with its wings and claws.

Perhaps the most famous firebird is the fabulous Phoenix of Ancient Egyptian, Phoenician, and later myths. Only one Phoenix lives at a time, although it lives for hundreds of years. At the end of its life, it builds a nest of sweet-smelling twigs. Both the nest and bird burn to ashes, from which a new, young Phoenix arises.

In Russian mythology, the Firebird is a large bird with glowing feathers. Finding a lost feather inspired many adventurers to capture a live bird. These quests traditionally caused these people great hardship for which they blamed the Firebird.

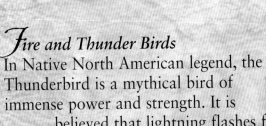

Images of the Thunderbird are popular in Native North American art and often appear carved on totem poles.

Prince Ivan returns from his quest on a magic carpet with a caged Firebird, by Viktor Vasnetsov.

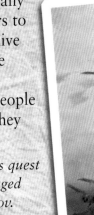

Eros

Since ancient times, human beings or humanlike creatures with wings have been featured in myths and legends. In Greek mythology, Eros is sometimes said to be the son of Ares, god of war, and Aphrodite, goddess of beauty. He is a charming but mischievous god who specializes in making people fall in love by piercing them with his golden arrows. He himself falls in love with a beautiful woman, called Psyche, when he grazes himself on one of his own arrows. In Roman mythology, Eros becomes Cupid. He is usually shown as a young boy, or sometimes a child, with his bow and arrows in hand.

Eros had two kinds of arrows. His golden arrows with dove feathers caused people to fall in love instantly. His lead arrows with owl feathers led to disinterest.

Hermes

Messengers of the Gods

Hermes is the Greek god who acts as a messenger between the gods of Mount Olympus and human beings. He is given this task by Apollo, to keep him out of trouble. He wears winged sandals and a winged helmet, to speed his flight between the worlds of the mortals and immortals. Hermes is also the protector of travelers and thieves. In Roman mythology, Mercury is the equivalent god.

Garuda

In the Hindu religion, Garuda is usually shown with the body of a man and the wings and beak of an eagle. He is the king of the birds, often chosen to carry the great god, Vishnu, and is the enemy of snakes and Nagas (see page 24). Garuda's story is told in the great Hindu sacred text, "The Mahabharata," in which he is a symbol of speed and military strength. Huge birds, also called Garudas, appear in the Buddhist religion. They are said to create hurricane-force winds when they flap their gigantic wings.

Worshipping Garuda is believed to cleanse the body of poisons.

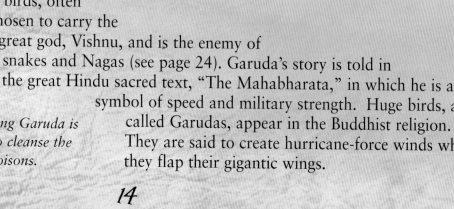

Angels

Angels are supernatural beings found in many religions. In Christianity, Islam, and Judaism, they are heavenly beings created by God, sent to Earth to instruct people about God's wishes or to perform other tasks. While angels are generally thought to be invisible to humans, they are often shown as humanlike creatures with varying pairs of wings. In Islamic belief, angels are made by Allah (God) from light but can take on any form they choose, human or otherwise. They are neither male nor female, and are immortal.

In the 17th-century painting by Guido Reni, the archangel Michael is shown in military dress as he fights against Satan.

Tengus

Tengus are spiritlike creatures that appear in Japanese folklore in many different forms. They are usually shown with both birdlike and human characteristics, including a bright red face and an extremely long nose. Tengus take their name from a fierce doglike demon in Chinese mythology that brought war and caused thunder. In early Japanese stories, they were enemies of Buddhism, kidnapping monks and robbing temples. They later returned their victims in a state of madness or near-death. In later tales, Tengus are divided into good and bad spirits. Some religious groups worshipped them as gods who protected sacred mountains and forests. In popular folk stories, Tengus are often portrayed as comical creatures who are easily tricked by humans. In one tale, a boy tricks a Tengu into exchanging its magic cloak of invisibility for a humble piece of bamboo.

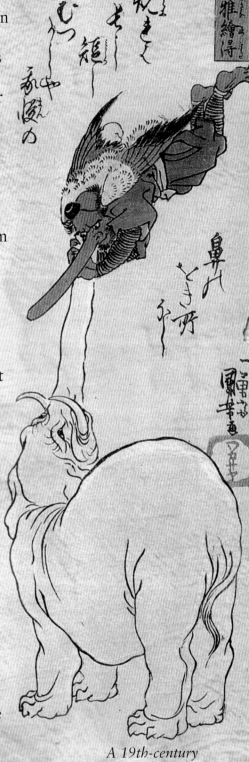

A 19th-century woodprint by Utagawa Kuniyoshi, showing an elephant catching a flying Tengu

A Leyak

Flying Heads

In the mythology of Bali, Leyaks are hideous flying creatures that haunt graveyards and feed on dead bodies. By day, they appear as ordinary humans. At night, their gruesome heads and internal organs break out of their bodies and fly.

One look from the Cockatrice can turn a person to stone. *16*

Chimera

Chimera are creatures made of the parts of different animals. The name comes from the Chimera of Greek mythology, a fire-breathing beast with the head and body of a lion, the head of a goat rising from its back, and the tail of a serpent.

The Chimera's father was Typhon, god of the wind, and its mother was Echidna, a monster who was part-woman, part-snake. It is eventually killed by Bellerophon, riding Pegasus, the winged horse (see page 11).

A stone plaque dating from around 1500 from a temple at Tepoztlan, south of Mexico City, which shows the Ahuizotl.

Mixed up Creatures

Many mythologies around the world feature the bizarre and outlandish Chimera. The Ahuizotl of Aztec myth is an extraordinary half-dog, half-monkey creature with a human hand on the end of its tail. It was believed to live near water, snatching people who ventured too close to the water's edge, or pulling fishermen from their boats. The Ahuizotl is greatly feared because of its fondness for eating human flesh.

In Japanese mythology, a Nue is a beast with a monkey's head, a raccoon dog's body, a tiger's legs, and a snake for a tail. It is said that a Nue can change itself into a black cloud and fly, bringing bad luck and illness.

A woodprint from 1852 showing a Nue, disguised as a black cloud, descending on the royal palace

One of the most feared Chimera is the Cockatrice. This dreaded creature resembles a large rooster, with dragon's wings and a serpent's tail. It was originally linked to another beast, called a Basilisk, although the Basilisk always takes the form of a snake. The Cockatrice's magic powers include a deadly stare that can kill people or turn them to stone. It can only be killed if its stare is reflected back at it from a polished surface, such as a mirror, or if it hears a rooster crow. The weasel, the Cockatrice's archenemy, is the only animal that can survive its gaze.

A 1642 woodblock print of a Basilisk (right)

The Good

Although most mythical creatures derive from our darkest fears, some originate from our "better" selves. The Unicorn of Western myth is one such legendary beast. A Unicorn is often portrayed as a white or grey horse-like creature with a single, spiral horn growing from its forehead. In the original myth, it was a Chimera made up of a horse, with a goat's cloven hooves and a lion's tail. It was thought to be a magical beast with healing powers. Its horn could detect poison in food and drink, and purify the poison to make it harmless. It is said that its horn was so valuable that the Unicorn was hunted to extinction. Although the Unicorn was a wild and formidable creature, hunters knew how to catch it. A maiden was used to enchant a Unicorn so that it fell asleep in her lap. Then the hunters cut off its horn.

It was said that only a gentle and pure maiden had the power to tame a Unicorn.

The Qilin from Chinese mythology is sometimes called the Chinese Unicorn, but it differs greatly in appearance (see right) and character. Despite its fearsome looks, it is a good omen, bringing peace or prosperity. It is so gentle that it can walk on grass yet not trample it or harm any insects. It is so peaceful that it does not eat meat. Even so, it can become fierce and breathe fire if it sees a wicked person threaten a good, pure person. In Japanese legend, the Qilin is called a Kirin. It looks more like a Western Unicorn than a Qilin does, but its body is covered in scales.

Japanese mythology also includes the Baku, another good Chimera. It is described in many different ways, combining parts of elephants, rhinos, and tigers. The Baku has long appeared in Japanese folk tales as a creature that devours people's nightmares.

A Japanese woodprint showing a Baku

Part-dragon, part-deer, and part-ox, the Chinese Qilin is also covered in scales.

20

Tales of Manticores are still told in parts of Asia. If a person disappears, it is believed that the Manticore has eaten them.

One kind of Ushi-oni is a huge, ferocious sea monster with the body of a crab and the head of a bull. It is said to live off the coast where it attacks fishermen.

The Bad...

Probably one of the scariest Chimeras is the Manticore. This legendary creature has the body of a lion and the head of a human, with three rows of savage, sharp teeth. It has the tail of a dragon or serpent that can shoot out poisonous spines or hairs to paralyze prey. This terrible beast is said to range in size from lion-sized to horse-sized. The Manticore originated in Persian mythology, where its name meant "man-eater." It is thought to kill its victims instantly with a bite or scratch, then to eat all of them, including their bones.

The Ushi-oni is another terrifying Chimera that appears in Japanese folklore. There are various kinds of Ushi-oni, but all of them are monstrous, with the horned heads of cattle. Tales are told of Ushi-oni who were persuaded to help farmers to plough their fields. They did the work amazingly fast but, of course, demanded their dues in the end...

The Tarasque is a fearsome monster that causes chaos and devastation across Provence, in France. Many knights tried and failed to capture it, until Saint Martha tamed it and led it back to the city where the people attacked and killed it.

Catoblepas

The Tarasque is a bizarre-looking Chimera with a lion's head, six bear-like legs, an ox-like body covered with a turtle's shell, and a scaly tail with a scorpion's stinger.

...And the Ugly

From Ethiopia comes a Chimera, called a Catoblepas. It is said to resemble a black buffalo, with a pig's head that is so large and heavy, it always hangs down to the ground. Trouble befalls anyone who comes across a Catoblepas. Like the Basilisk (see page 17), its stare and breath are deadly, killing people or turning them to stone.

Centaurs carrying off nymphs.

Half-human, half-beast

Strange-looking creatures composed of unexpected combinations of animal and human features have appeared throughout mythology since ancient times. They are shown as animals with human heads or torsos, or as humans with animal heads.

The famous Centaur Chiron was a wise teacher of Greek heroes, including Achilles.

An Onocentaur, with the top half of a human and the body of a donkey

Centaurs

Half-horse, half-human, Centaurs first appeared in Ancient Greek mythology. They are the sons or grandsons of Ixion, king of the Lapiths, and the goddess, Nephele, whom Zeus created out of clouds. Centaurs are caught between two natures. They may be as wild and untameable as horses, but they are also as wise and brave as human teachers. They are often shown carrying off nymphs, when their wild side dominates. Female Centaurs, called Kentaurides, appear in later Greek and Roman myths. The Onocentaur, a creature with a human top half and a donkey's body appeared in later myths.

Centaurs from Mesopotamia

Centaur-like creatures are also found in the ancient myths of Mesopotamia. The Urmahlullu, or "lion-man," is a guardian spirit with the body of a lion and the head and torso of a human. Centaurs with lions' bodies also appear in English heraldry, as seen in the emblems of the 12th-century King Stephen.

Several Mesopotamian myths feature Centaurs with the bodies of scorpions. In the famous epic of Gilgamesh, they stand guard outside the gates to the land of the sun god, Shamash. They open the gates as the sun god rises.

In Mesopotamia, statues of the Urmahlullu stood outside the rooms where the priests ritually washed.

Scorpion men are called Aqrabuamelu or Girtablilu. It is said that they were created by the sea goddess, Tiamat, to wage war against the other gods.

23

Snake People

In Hindu stories, Nagas are serpent gods that play an important part in religion. They often appear as half-human, half-snake, or as snakes with multiple heads, each one hooded like a cobra's. Nagas are associated with water, protecting wells and rivers, and controlling life-giving rainclouds. Hugely powerful, their only enemy is the giant bird-man, Garuda (see page 14). Tales about Nagas are also commonly found in Buddhist stories, where a Naga, called Mucalinda, uses its hood to shelter the Buddha from a great storm. Chinese tales tell of Nuwa, a creature that is half-woman, half-snake. She is said to have created humans out of lumps of clay, and to have repaired the sky after a terrible catastrophe destroyed the world.

Nuwa and her husband, Fuxi

A female Naga is called a Nagini. Legend says that Nagas are dangerous to humans but only if they have been provoked or angered.

Satyrs and Fauns

The Satyrs of Greek mythology are woodland creatures who are human down to the waist, apart from pointed ears and horns, but with a goat's hairy legs and hooves. They are the pleasure-loving followers of Pan, the god of shepherds and hunting, who is often shown playing pipes. Their favorite occupations are drinking wine and chasing nymphs. Their counterparts in Roman myths are known as Fauns.

A similar half-human creature from Greek legend is an Ipotane. Its name means "horse-person" and it is shown as having a horse's hindquarters, legs, and tail, with the head and upper body of a human.

An Ipotane

Pan's music can inspire people or cause panic, depending on his intentions (right).

24

The Minotaur

The famous Minotaur of Greek mythology is a terrible monster with the body of a man and the head of a huge bull. His father is a white bull sent to King Minos of Crete by Poseidon, the sea god. His mother is Pasiphae, the human wife of King Minos. The Minotaur is trapped deep inside the mazelike Labyrinth, which Minos has built to contain him. There he lived until he was killed by the Athenian hero Theseus, who was sent into the Labyrinth as a sacrifice. Theseus finds his way out of the Labyrinth by using a ball of thread given to him by Minos's daughter, Ariadne.

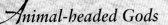

In Greek, Minotaur means "Bull of Minos." The historical site of Knossos in Crete is thought to be the site of the Labyrinth.

Animal-headed Gods

Many cultures around the world worship deities with animal heads. In the Hindu religion, Ganesha, the elephant-headed god, is one of the best-known and most honored gods. He is believed to remove obstacles and is worshipped at the beginning of every new task. Most stories tell how Ganesha, the son of the goddess Parvati and the great god Shiva, is born with a human head and body. Later, however, Shiva beheads him in a quarrel. Shiva then replaces Ganesha's original head with that of an elephant.

In the mythology and religion of Ancient Egypt, many gods were portrayed with the heads of animals. Two of the most well known are Bastet who has the head of a cat, and Sobek, who has the head of a crocodile.

An ancient name for Ganesha is "Ekadanta" or "One-tusked." This refers to the fact that he has only one whole tusk, the other having broken off.

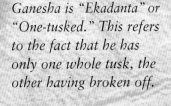

The Ancient Egyptian gods, Bastet and Sobek

Dog-headed

A dog-headed human is called a Cynocephalus. These creatures are featured in many medieval writings. They are often used to depict people from distant lands who appeared outlandish to early explorers.

An illustration of a Cynocephalus from a 15th-century book

A Kraken attacks sailors and their ship.

Water Beasts

Some of the largest creatures in mythology are water beasts, in particular those that live in the oceans. Reports from sailors, even today, tell of strange and fearsome monsters that attack them and their ships.

A boatful of unfortunate sailors land on the Aspidochelone's back.

Sea Serpents and other Monsters of the Deep

Sea serpents appear in many mythologies, especially those of maritime countries. Some people believe that these monsters are actual sea creatures, such as whales or sharks, exaggerated in size by frightened sailors. Others think they might actually exist, being surviving examples of prehistoric sea reptiles. Whatever their origins, sea serpents are usually gigantic creatures.

The Aspidochelone, known from medieval texts, is supposed to have been the size of an island. In Norse mythology, Jormungandr (see page 9) is so long, its body can encircle the entire world. In 1848, a serpent about 65 feet long (20 meters) was reportedly sighted by the crew of *HMS Daedalus* while on an Atlantic voyage.

The Leviathan is a biblical sea creature whose name has come to mean any enormous, whale-like sea creature. In one legend, the Leviathan devours one whale a day. Later reports claim that it is able to swallow large ships.

In his book, History of the Northern Peoples, *16th-century Swedish writer Olaus Magnus describes many sea monsters such as this serpent.*

The Kraken

The legendary Kraken of Scandinavian mythology is another enormous sea monster, with immense tentacles. Sailors not only feared the monster itself but the powerful whirlpool it created when it suddenly descended into the sea. Even the largest ships could be sucked into the deadly whirlpool. The story of the Kraken may have originated from sightings of a real giant squid.

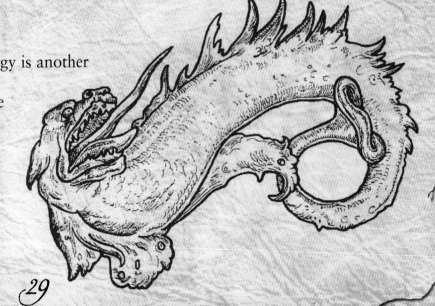

An artist's impression of the biblical Leviathan

Scylla and Charybdis

In Greek mythology, Scylla and Charybdis are terrifying monsters that guard the opposite sides of a strait (channel of water). The channel is so narrow that it is impossible for sailors to navigate safely between the two. Scylla is a grotesque sea monster with six snapping heads and a ring of snarling dogs around her waist. Originally a sea nymph, Charybdis takes the form of a gigantic whirlpool that sucks ships down to their doom. According to Homer's *Odyssey*, the hero, Odysseus, is one of the very few to successfully navigate the channel by sailing closer to Scylla, even though the monster kills six of his men.

When Scylla kills Odysseus's men, the hero takes the oars and helps row the ship to safety through the strait.

Sea Horses and Sea Lions

Hippocampus is the Greek word for the tiny and unusual fish, known as the seahorse. In Greek mythology, however, it is a huge creature with the body of a horse and the tail of a fish or dolphin that pulls the chariot of Poseidon, god of the sea. The Etruscan legends speak of fish-tailed lions called Leopkampai, fish-tailed bulls called Taurokampoi, and fish-tailed leopards known as Pardalokampai.

Leocampus and Hippocampus

The Nuckelavee

The Nuckelavee

A terrible sea monster, the Nuckelavee is found in Celtic mythology. This hideous creature has legs that are partly finned and a horse's body with a human head and torso growing out of its back. Its enormous mouth gapes open, and its single eye burns with a red flame. Even more grusomely, the beast has no skin on its body. The Nuckelavee lives mainly in the sea but cannot cross running water, such as rivers and streams. It occasionally rampages across the land, spreading plague and causing crops to die.

Lake Monsters

Over many centuries, there have been numerous reports of huge animals living in lakes around the world. The most famous lake monster is the Loch Ness Monster, or "Nessie," thought to inhabit Loch Ness in Scotland. Similar monsters have been widely reported in North America, such as Ogopogo in Okanagan Lake in British Columbia; Champ in Lake Champlain on the United States and Canadian border; and Manipogo in Lake Manitoba in Canada.

The Loch Ness Monster

Bunyips, Kappas, and Kelpies

According to Australian aboriginal legend, the Bunyip, a large, fearsome devil, lurks in rivers, creeks, lakes, and swamps. It is sometimes described as having a doglike face, dark fur, a horselike tail, flippers, and tusks like a walrus. Its bloodcurdling roar can be heard for miles around, as it lies in wait for its prey.

Small children are one of the Kappa's favorite meals, although they will also eat adults (below).

Water spirits, called Kappas, are said to haunt rivers and ponds in Japan. They have scaly skin, webbed feet, and are able to swim like fish. The Kelpie is a mythological water horse from Scotland. It lures a human onto its back, then dives into the deepest lake and drowns its unfortunate victim.

In Scandinavian mythology, Kelpies are known as brook horses (below).

A Bunyip creeping out of a swamp.

Giants

Monsters of enormous size and strength appear in many of the world's myths and legends. The English word for these colossal beings is "Giant," derived from one of the most famous ancient examples, the Gigantes of Greek mythology.

The Gigantes

In Ancient Greece, the Gigantes are the giant children of Gaia, goddess of the Earth, and Uranus, god of the sky. Furious that another group of her children, the Titans, has been imprisoned by the gods of Mount Olympus, Gaia encourages the Gigantes to wage war against the Olympians. The fierce battle that follows is sometimes known as the Gigantomachy.

Led by Alcyoneus and Porphyrion, the Gigantes attempt to reach the top of Mount Olympus by stacking three other mountain ranges on top of each other. The Olympians call on the hero, Heracles (see page 37) for help. He kills Alcyoneus, then strikes down Porphyrion with an arrow, after Zeus hits him with a lightning bolt.

Soon the gods' defeat of the Gigantes is complete. The gods once more take control of the world and condemn the Gigantes to the underworld.

Atlas is the leader of the Titans who lost a war with the Olympian gods. Zeus condemns him to stand on the edge of the world and hold up the sky on his shoulders.

An ancient carving from India depicting the goddess Durga doing battle with the Daityas

Other Warring Giants

In other mythologies, giants are creatures of chaos who are frequently in conflict with the gods. In Hinduism there are giants called Daityas who also fight the gods, with varying degrees of success. In Norse mythology, the Jotuns often do battle with the gods, even though many are related to them by marriage. These battles grow fiercer over time, and at the final battle of Ragnarok, the Jotuns storm Asgard and kill most of the gods. Ymir is another important Norse giant from whose body the world was created. Odin and his brothers used Ymir's flesh to create the earth. The blood of Ymir formed seas and lakes.

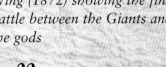

A painting by Marten Eskil Wing (1872) showing the final battle between the Giants and the gods

The giants of Irish mythology were called the Formorians.

The Formorians

Irish mythology has tales of warlike giants called the Formorians. These creatures represent the forces of chaos and nature, as opposed to the Tuatha De Danaan, who were a wise race of magical, godlike people. Legend tells how the Formorians fight off waves of settlers who come to live in Ireland but they are eventually defeated by the Tuatha De Danaan at the second Battle of Magh Tuireadh. The Formorians are led by Balor, a giant with an evil eye that kills anything caught in its gaze. In the battle, the half-Formorian Lug kills Balor, then drives the defeated giants into the sea.

The Giant's Causeway in northeast Ireland is said to have been built by the giant, Fionn mac Cumhaill.

Giant Stones

A Jentil building an ancient monument.

In many cultures, legends tell how giants shape the landscape. The frost giants of Norse mythology are said to have carved out the rivers, valleys, and fjords. They were born from the sweat of Ymir (see page 33), the first living being, and lived in Niflheim, the land of ice. The great god Odin killed Ymir and used his bones and teeth to make the rocks and mountains. The Giant's Causeway in Northern Ireland is built by the giant, Fionn mac Cumhaill.

In Basque mythology (the Basques are a people from southwest France and north-central Spain), a race of giants called the Jentil, or Jentilak, live alongside humans. They are very hairy, very tall, and they can walk across the sea. They are so strong that they can hurl huge rocks down from the mountains where they live. This ability is said to explain the ancient stone monuments and standing stones found in the region.

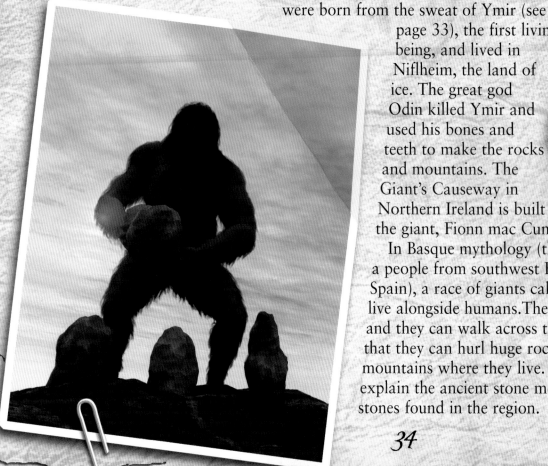

One-eyed Giants

In Greek mythology, the Cyclops are enormously strong giants, with one eye in the middle of their foreheads. They make the weapons of the gods, and fight for the gods against the Titans. The Cyclops live as shepherds on an island of the same name.

Homer's *Odyssey* tells the story of the hero Odysseus's journey home after the Trojan War. On his way, Odysseus and his men land on the island of Cyclops where the giant, Polyphemus, imprisons them in his cave and begins to eat them, one by one. Odysseus uses a stick to blind Polyphemus as he sleeps, allowing him and his men to escape when the blind giant lets his sheep out of the cave. Odysseus and his men cling to the underside of the sheep to flee.

A Cyclops tends his flock of sheep.

A Troll rests in a forest.

Trolls

The Trolls of Scandinavian folklore and fairytales are enormously strong and ugly creatures who come out of their caves at nighttime to hunt for human prey. Although dressed like human beings, they sometimes have a tail hidden inside their clothing. They possess magical powers that they use to cause mischief and harm. Often invisible, they can also take the shape of animals and trees.

Ogres

Unlike other giants, which may be good or bad, Ogres are always cruel. These vicious monsters feed on human beings. They are first mentioned in fairytales from the 17th century and have since appeared in many works of literature. In art, Ogres are usually shown with immensely strong bodies, large heads, and bushy beards. Ogres appear as villains in modern literature, films, and video games. Although they are dangerous, they can be easily tricked.

In this painting by Italian artist Giovanni Lanfanco, a man and woman are terrorized by a gigantic Ogre.

35

Rock Hurler

The legendary Irish hero Fionn mac Cumhail (Finn McCool) is also known as a giant. There are many stories about his life and adventures. Among them is the tale of how Fionn and his teacher, Finneces, catch the "salmon of knowledge." Fionn accidentally eats some of the salmon skin, gaining all the knowledge in the world.

Fionn is also held responsible for carving out many features of the landscape. He built the Giant's Causeway (see page 34) as a roadway to Scotland. Fionn also created the Isle of Man by tearing up part of Ireland and hurling it at a rival. It missed his foe and landed in the sea, becoming an isle. The empty space left behind became Lough Neagh, the largest lake in the British Isles.

Fionn mac Cumhail hurled part of Ireland into the Irish Sea, creating the Isle of Man. A smaller rock became the island of Rockall.

Talking Heads

In Welsh mythology, Bran the Blessed is a giant and a great king of Britain. His story is told in an ancient collection of tales, called the Mabinogion. Bran and his army fight the Irish over the mistreatment of Branwen, Bran's sister. The Welsh win the war, but only seven of their men survive. They include Bran, who is mortally wounded. He orders his men to cut off his head and bury it in London. His head continues to talk to the men throughout the following years.

Legend says that Bran's head is buried where the Tower of London stands today.

Hero Giants

In Homer's *Iliad*, the Greek hero and warrior Ajax is described as being immensely tall, strong, and brave in battle. During the Trojan War, Ajax is chosen to fight the Trojan hero, Hector. Later, he quarrels with Odysseus over Achilles' armor and kills himself in shame.

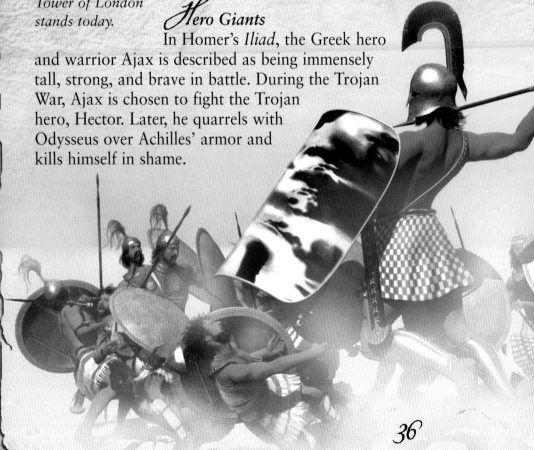

Ajax is the most famous of the Greek warriors. He goes into battle, wielding a huge spear and bearing a great shield made from seven ox-hides, and a layer of bronze. When Achilles is killed, Ajax uses a huge hammer to fight off the Trojans so that he and Odysseus can get Achilles' body and take it safely back to their camp for burial.

Wrestling Matches

Antaeus, a giant of Greek myth, is the son of the gods Gaia and Poseidon. As long as he remains in contact with the ground, he will never lose his amazing strength. To collect human skulls for a temple he is building to honor his father, Antaeus challenges everyone he meets to a wrestling match—to the death. Antaeus is always victorious until he meets his match in Heracles. Discovering the secret of Antaeus's power, Heracles uses his wits to defeat the giant. Knowing he can't beat Antaeus by throwing him to the ground, Heracles lifts the giant into the air and crushes him in a bear hug.

Heracles crushing the giant, Antaeus, to death

Biblical Giants

One of the best-known encounters between a giant and a human appears in the Bible (Book of Samuel). In a battle between the Israelites and the Philistines, the giant Philistine warrior, Goliath, appears every day to challenge the Israelites to single combat. No one takes up the offer as they are too afraid. Eventually, David, a shepherd boy and future king of Israel, steps forward. Refusing armor, David approaches Goliath, armed only with a sling and a few stones. He kills the giant with a stone, then cuts off its head.

A 19th-century painting showing the battle between David and the giant, Goliath

Earth-shaking Giants

According to Maya legends, earthquakes are caused by the giant, Cabracan, shaking the mountains by tapping them with his foot. To protect Earth, the twin gods, Hunahpu and Xbalanque, set out on a quest to defeat the giant. The twins fool the giant into thinking that they are simply mountain hunters. They offer to lead the giant to a mountain they had discovered where he can show off his powers. On the way, they trick him into eating a poisoned bird, which robs him of his strength. His legs feel so weak that he cannot even lift his feet.

Hunahpu and Xbalanque meet the mountain-shaking giant, Cabracan.

A modern Werewolf transforming from human to wolf 38

Shape-Shifters

An 18th-century German woodcut of a Werewolf shape-shifting

Almost every culture around the world has myths about shape-shifting. While the popular idea of a shape-shifter is of a human who magically transforms into an animal, there are numerous stories about animals that can also transform themselves.

In Central and South America, the Were-jaguar is the most usual were-animal.

Werewolves

Throughout northern Europe and North America, we find legends of Werewolves, humans who turn into ferocious, man-eating wolves. This transformation usually takes place during a full moon. A person becomes a Werewolf by either being bitten by another Werewolf or by falling under a curse. One way to kill a Werewolf is with a weapon made from silver, such as a bullet or a knife. A Werewolf always shifts back into human shape just before it dies.

Perhaps the most famous Vampire, Count Dracula appeared in the 1897 novel by Bram Stoker.

Shape-shifters similar to Werewolves are found in many myths. Most of them involve humans transforming into animals other than wolves. In Indian mythology there is a were-tiger, a sorcerer who's known to prey on livestock and might, at any time, turn to eating people, instead, as its prey.

Vampires

In both ancient and modern legends, vampires are living corpses who pierce their victims' skin with their terrifying fangs and suck their blood. Vampires are active only at night. As daylight approaches, they must return to the safety of their coffins. They can shape-shift between human and other animal forms, such as a bat.

A Navajo Yeenaaldlooshi is usually shown wearing only a coyote skin or wolf skin.

A Strigoi rises from its grave.

Souls of the Dead

In Romanian mythology, Strigoi are evil souls of the dead that rise from their graves at night. They transform into animals or ghosts and haunt the countryside, terrorizing anyone they meet. They are said to be closely related to Werewolves (see page 39).

Selkies and Swan Maidens

Some shape-shifters use an article of clothing or a layer of skin to change forms. The Selkie of Scottish legend can transform themselves from seals into humans. To do this, they must remove their seal skins. They must put them back on to turn into animals again. Sometimes humans hide the seal skins, forcing the Selkies to remain in human form. Likewise, the Swan Maidens of Norse legend must wear a magical robe of swan feathers in order to shape-shift from humans into swans.

Swan Maidens bathing

A Selkie reaches for her seal skin.

40

Skinwalkers and Wendigos

Some Native American myths tell of shape-shifting Skinwalkers, humans who are able to transform themselves into any animal they wish. One of the best-known Skinwalkers is the Yeenaaldlooshii of Navajo legend. It is most commonly seen as a wolf, coyote, owl, crow, or fox. Skinwalkers are greatly feared because they attack humans and can steal a person's skin, or soul, by staring into a person's eyes.

From the Native Americans who lived in colder, harsher climates comes the chilling legend of the Wendigo. In many versions of this tale, a human, after some act of cannibalism, is transformed into a creature that voraciously feeds on human flesh. Doomed to an eternal hunger, the Wendigo can never get its fill. The only way to stop the monster is to kill it by melting its frozen heart.

A 19th-century print, showing the Japanese Prince Hanzoku being tormented by a Kitsune

Many-tailed Foxes

Foxlike creatures often appear in Japanese mythology. They are known as Kitsune, and are said to be wise and intelligent. The more tails a Kitsune has, the wiser it is said to be. Kitsune also possess magical powers. Among these is the ability to change shape and transform themselves into humans.

Egyptian gods, Horus and Seth

Shape-Shifting Gods

In various mythologies, deities use their power to change shape. Egyptian myths tell how the god Seth changes into a pig, and then a hippo, before being defeated by Horus. In Greek legend, Zeus shape-shifts on several occasions to win the attention of mortal women. He appears to Europa as a white bull, to Leda as a swan, and to Danae as a shower of gold.

Europa is carried off by Zeus, disguised as a white bull.

A demon bursts from the depths of Hell.

Demons, Ghouls, & Ghosts

Creatures that represent evil and darkness are an important concept in many religions, cultures, and folklores. The opposite of goodness and purity, demons and ghouls terrorize people, and witches are often considered malevolent.

Demons come in many forms, such as Buer (above), the demon leader with a lion's head and five goats' legs surrounding his body.

Demons

Demons are prominent figures in many religions, and they often appear remarkably similar from culture to culture. They are often found opposing the gods, God, or forces of good. In Hindu religion, demons are evil beings called Rakshasas, who are in constant battle against the gods. In Christianity, demons are considered to be angels who fell from favor by rebelling against God. They are the cause of evil and ignorance in the world. Their leader is commonly known as the Devil, or Satan. In Japanese folklore, Oni are gigantic demons with sharp claws, fangs, and two horns growing out of their heads. They are often shown carrying a club and dressed in tiger skin. Their skin is usually red or blue. Oni may originally have been evil spirits who caused disease and disaster. In some parts of Japan, festivals were held each year to drive the Oni away. Recently, the Oni have been given a role of protector and are believed to ward off bad luck.

A ferocious-looking Rakshasa appears in a temple painting (above). A statue of an Oni brandishing a club (below).

In different cultures, the Devil has different names, including Abbadon, Angra Mainyu, Satan, Asmodai, Beelzebub, Lucifer, Belias, and Iblis.

Gargoyles and Grotesques

A Gargoyle is a stone carving used to decorate buildings and has a spout for carrying rain water away from the building. A Grotesque is similar but does not have a waterspout. Gargoyles are often monsters or demonlike creatures, and they are believed to protect a building from evil spirits.

This Gargoyle appears on Notre Dame Cathedral in Paris, France.

Djinn

In Islam, Djinn are invisible beings created by Allah (God) from fire. They can be either good or evil, having the same free will as human beings. They are thought to live in places that are unclean and to cause fear and confusion when they meddle in human affairs. Sometimes, they attempt to take over people's bodies. Shaitan, or Iblis, is the chief of the Djinns. He disobeys Allah and becomes the enemy of humans, seeking to turn them away from Allah.

Fantastical Djinns, or Genies, are found in folktales from Arabia, Persia, and India, most notably in the book *The Arabian Nights*. In the story of Aladdin, a Djinn imprisoned in an old brass lamp is set free by the young boy's mother. The Djinn rewards Aladdin with riches and power.

A ghoul raids a desert graveyard.

Zombies are popular in modern horror films.

Ghoul

In ancient Arabian legends, a ghoul, or gul, is a monstrous demon that can take the shape of an animal, especially a dog or hyena. It lives in the desert and lures travelers into its den where it kills and eats them. It also haunts graveyards where it opens graves and feasts on the dead. In European literature, ghouls live among the undead, alongside zombies (see below). Once human, these hideous creatures live off human flesh and cannot tolerate sunlight. Traditionally, ghouls could be driven away by the ringing of church bells.

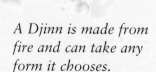

Zombies

Zombies are corpses that have been brought back to life. They originated on the island of Haiti where they play an important part in Voodoo beliefs. They are revived by a sorcerer and remain under his control because they have no free will of their own. In modern horror films, Zombies are usually shown as hideous, flesh-eating creatures whose bodies are decomposing. They often travel together in groups, terrorizing towns and villages.

A Djinn is made from fire and can take any form it chooses.

Hags, Witches, and Banshees

Hags appear in myths and folk tales from around the world and are generally depicted as wizened old women. The word "hag" may come from an old English word for witch. Though sometimes viewed as good and fairylike, Hags are often considered malevolent, causing nightmares (see below), and frightening children. One famous and hideous Hag is Baba Yaga, who appears in many Eastern European myths. She is said to fly around in a giant mortar (a bowl used for grinding spices and herbs), using a pestle (grinder) as a paddle. She lives deep in the forest in a log cabin that stands on chicken's legs, surrounded by a fence of spikes, each with a human skull on top. Most stories tell how she kidnaps children, her favorite food, and brings about storms and tempests. A few stories tell a different tale, however, of how Baba Yaga helps people who are lost or on a quest.

In Irish mythology, a Banshee is a female spirit, or fairy, who is seen as a bringer of death. Her wailing voice can be heard if someone is about to die. Some families, especially noble ones, were said to have Banshees associated with them. Banshees are often described as wearing white or grey, with long, fair hair.

A painting of Baba Yaga

A Banshee may wail softly for a peaceful death; more loudly for a violent one.

The three witches from Shakespeare's Macbeth, illustrated by Arthur Rackham

The Stuff of Nightmares

A Mara, or Mare, is a female demon from Scandinavian mythology. Mares are said to move about at night, entering rooms through keyholes or under the door. They crouch on the chest of someone sleeping, causing bad dreams. The word "nightmare" comes from these demons.

The Nightmare, painted by Henry Fuseli in 1781

45

Glossary

Aboriginal
Referring to the Aborigines, the original inhabitants of Australia who arrived there thousands of years ago.

Arthurian
Stories relating to the time of King Arthur, a legendary British king.

Beneficial
Something good or positive.

Benevolent
Helpful, friendly, or kindly.

Caiman
A reptile related to alligators and crocodiles.

Coyote
A doglike animal that lives in the deserts and prairies of North America.

Deity
A god or goddess.

Extinct
A plant or animal that has died out and can never exist again.

Fjord
A long, narrow inlet of the ocean between steep, high cliffs, commonly found in Norway.

Folklore
The stories, customs, and beliefs of a people or culture that describe events that happened in the past.

Heraldic
Relating to heraldry, the use of images, decorations, and colors to represent a ruler, an important person or a family. Heraldic symbols were originally used on armor, flags, and shields.

Hero
A mythological being with great strength and ability, often half-mortal, half-god.

Hoards
A large collection of something, such as a dragon's treasure.

Icon
A religious image, painted on wood and displayed in some Eastern European churches.

Iliad
A great Ancient Greek poem, said to have been composed by Homer in the 8th or 9th centuries BC. The work is based on the legend of the Trojan War.

Immortality
Never dying, but living forever.

Invulnerable
Not able to be wounded or hurt.

Legend

A traditional story that is often based on supposedly historical events. Like myths, legends were originally passed down by word of mouth by storytellers.

Malevolent

Wishing evil on others; another word for malicious.

Manatee

A large, air-breathing sea mammal, sometimes called a sea cow. Reports of Mermaid sightings may actually have been of manatees.

Maritime

Relating to the sea.

Millennia

A millennium (singular) is a thousand years.

Medieval

Relating to the Middle Ages, a period of European history that lasted from around the 5th century to the 15th century AD.

Myth

A traditional story, not based in historical fact but using supernatural characters to explain human behavior and natural events. Myths helped ancient people to understand the world around them.

Nymph

In Greek mythology, a nymph was a spirit of nature who appeared as a beautiful girl.

Odyssey

A great Ancient Greek poem, said to have been composed by Homer in the 8th or 9th centuries BC. It tells of the adventures of the hero Odysseus as he returned from the Trojan War.

Quest

In medieval legends, an expediton by a knight or group of knights to accomplish a task, such as the search for a mythical beast.

Quetzal

A bird from Central America that has beautiful red and green plumage. Its feathers were highly prized by the Aztecs and other peoples of the region.

Sacrifice

An animal or human that is killed and offered to the gods or goddesses in order to win their favor.

Sorcerer

A person who uses magical powers.

Strait

A narrow channel of seawater that connects two larger bodies of water.

Supernatural

Magical beings, such as fairies, ghosts and gods, and events that cannot be explained by physical or scientific laws.

Torso

The trunk, or top part, of a human body.

Voodoo

A religion that is practiced mainly on the Caribbean island of Haiti.

Index